NATURE'S WRATH
THE SCIENCE BEHIND NATURAL DISASTERS

THE SCIENCE OF
AVALANCHES

RICHARD SPILSBURY

Gareth Stevens
Publishing

Please visit our website, www.garethstevens.com. For a free color catalog of all our
high-quality books, call toll free 1-800-542-2595 or fax 1-877-542-2596.

Publisher Cataloging Data

Spilsbury, Richard, 1963-
        The science of avalanches / Richard Spilsbury.
p.   cm. – (Nature's wrath : the science behind natural disasters)
Includes bibliographical references and index.
Summary: This book describes different types of avalanche, conditions that can
cause an avalanche, the tools scientists use to predict where an avalanche may occur, and more.
Contents: Types of avalanche – What causes avalanches? – Avalanche impacts –
Controlling avalanches.
        ISBN 978-1-4339-8651-2 (hard bound) – ISBN 978-1-4339-8652-9 (pbk.)
ISBN 978-1-4339-8653-6 (6-pack)
        1. Avalanches—Juvenile literature   [1. Avalanches]   I. Title
                2013
        551.3/07—dc23

First Edition

Published in 2013 by
Gareth Stevens Publishing
111 East 14th Street, Suite 349
New York, NY 10003

© 2013 Gareth Stevens Publishing

Produced by Calcium, www.calciumcreative.co.uk
Designed by Simon Borrough and Nick Leggett
Edited by Sarah Eason and Vicky Egan
Picture research by Susannah Jayes

Photo credits: Cover: Top: Shutterstock: My Good Images; Bottom (l to r): Dreamstime:
Jdazuelos, Brett Pelletier, Amidala76, Shutterstock: Tobias Machhaus, Dreamstime: Trombax;
Inside: ABS Avalanche Airbag: 33cl; Dreamstime: Auddmin 44c, Bb226 4r, Tom Dowd 31b,
Anna Dudko 1c, 7, Neil Harrison 22c, Janthonjackson 20cl, Komelau 28tr, Monkey Business
Images 6tr, Peter Montgomery 11tr, Nikittta 39t, Noamfein 12-13tc, Pxlxl 8r, Anna Rutkovskaya
15c, Malgorzata Slusarczyk 38c, Yulan 29c; NASA: Created by Jesse Allen, Earth Observatory,
using data obtained from the University of Maryland's Global Land Cover Facility 20-21tc;
Shutterstock: Nate A. 18c, amidala76 35t, Galyna Andrushko 11cl, 12-13c, Andrew Arseev
27, Alexander Chaikin 43t, deepspacedave 1b, 23cl, 35cr, Loris Eichenberger 34cr, Elnur 45b,
Timothy Epp 14b, Gts 25c, Péter Gudella 26tr, Vladislav Gurfinkel 36tr, Jaxatoan 32cr, Falk
Kienas 33cr, Vladimir Melnik 21bl, Dominik Michalek 24c, Maxim Petrichuk 19t, Roca 30cr,
salajean 5c, scattoselvaggio 9b, Joyce Sherwin 16tr, smereka 17, Martin Trajkovski 42cr; US
Geological Survey: Erich Peitzsch 37; Wikipedia: Jossy89 41c, Tim 40c.

Printed in the United States of America

CPSIA compliance information: Batch #CW13GS: For further information contact Gareth Stevens, New York, New York at 1-800-542-2595.

CONTENTS

WHAT IS AN AVALANCHE?

An avalanche is a sudden, massive fall of snow, ice, and rocks down a steep mountainside. Avalanches can fall rapidly and can travel long distances downhill if they start high up on a steep-sided mountain. As the snow falls, it makes a loud, rumbling sound similar to a freight train.

Most avalanches happen in remote areas and do not pose a threat to anyone.

Sliding Snow

An avalanche starts when a slab of snow or ice on a mountainside breaks away from the soil or rock beneath. As it shifts, it knocks into more snow, and in a short space of time, a large quantity of snow and ice is on the move, picking up soil, rocks, and trees as it slides down the side of the mountain.

4

Small Avalanches

How dangerous an avalanche is depends on its size, speed, and location. Once snow starts moving, it builds up speed, so even a small avalanche can knock a person off their feet. A small avalanche would have little impact in remote hills where no one is living, but in a ski resort it could bury a party of skiers alive.

Avalanches can bury cars and buildings in an instant.

Destructive Force

A large avalanche is one of the deadliest forces of nature. It is almost impossible to outrun, and the weight of the wall of snow crushes everything beneath it. Avalanches destroy anything in their paths, from forests and houses to entire towns. Today, scientists study avalanches carefully to help people prepare for and prevent such disasters from happening.

WORLD'S WORST

In 1970, an earthquake in Peru caused a piece of glacier to break off and slide downhill. The ice was 1 mile (1.6 km) wide and weighed millions of tons. It pushed ahead of it a wave of snow and soil that was 3,000 feet (910 m) high. The avalanche buried the town of Yungay in the valley below, killing 25,000 people.

CHAPTER ONE
TYPES OF AVALANCHE

Avalanches occur on slopes in countries and regions where lots of snow falls each year. They happen frequently in these places and come in all shapes and sizes. There are three main types: Sluff avalanches, slab avalanches, and wet avalanches.

SLUFF AVALANCHES

A sluff avalanche can happen after a snowfall of small, powdery snowflakes land on a mountain slope. The snow either falls on rock or on an older layer of snow, called a "snowpack." A snowpack is a hard layer of snow that has been squashed by the pressure of snow on top, making it pack together like a snowball. Unlike heavy, wet snowflakes, loose, dry snowflakes do not stick together and are easily dislodged by the wind. As soon as they start to roll downhill, they knock into other loose snowflakes, which in turn start to roll. Within a few seconds, a fan-shaped avalanche that grows wider as it moves can form. Sluff avalanches are not often deadly because they do not carry a great deal of snow with them. However, they do often injure skiers and snowboarders by pushing them over cliffs or ridges on steep mountain slopes.

Skiers and snowboarders that ski on steep slopes with dry, powdery snow risk becoming caught in a sluff avalanche.

WORLD'S WORST

In 218 BC, the Carthaginian military commander Hannibal led an army from Spain through France and across the Alps into northern Italy. A devastating avalanche struck while he was crossing the Alps, killing around 18,000 of his men.

Many sluff avalanches happen in high, rocky mountains where lots of powdery snow falls.

SLIDING SLABS

If you lifted a table at one end, a dinner plate would slide straight down it. The weight of the plate pulls it down the slope, and it builds up speed as it travels, especially if the plate is heavy. The same can happen with snow. Sometimes, a large slab of snow breaks away and slides down a mountainside, picking up speed as it travels. This is called a slab avalanche.

Stuck Together

The slab is a thick layer of snow in which the flakes are firmly stuck together. Sometimes slabs of snow lie on top of a weaker layer of snow. If the weaker layer collapses under the weight of the slab, it can cause the heavy slab to slide. The weak layer is more likely to collapse if the snow that formed it fell quickly. If 20 inches (50 cm) of snow falls in a week, the weak layer has time to adjust gradually to the weight of new snow. But if 20 inches (50 cm) falls in just a couple of hours, the weak layer is likely to give way under the sudden increase in the slab's weight.

Slab avalanches are the most common type of avalanche. This one has exposed underlying rock.

Shattering Snow

The slab of snow is stronger than the snow underneath, but it is also quite brittle. As it slides, it shatters into jagged pieces a little like broken glass. Each of the pieces can weigh many tons, and they slide like a sled over the slippery snow beneath. A slab avalanche can reach speeds of 80 miles (130 km) per hour within 5 seconds of first moving. That is faster than a cheetah can sprint after its prey!

A freak storm in February 2010 produced a massive snowfall in mountains near Kabul, Afghanistan. A series of 32 avalanches struck, killing at least 172 people and blocking a major route north of the city. More than 2,500 people were trapped in their cars for days.

Weak layers of snow can cover large areas. Once one part collapses, the snow around it then collapses, too. This creates a domino effect, and a large slab of snow starts to slide downhill.

9

REAL-LIFE SCIENCE
MOUNT KANG GURU,
Nepal, 2005

In October 2005, a team of climbers and guides set out to climb Mount Kang Guru, which is 22,903 feet (6,981 m)—almost 4.3 miles (7 km)—high. The mountain is a challenging climb, with lots of steep, sharp ridges, but the climbers were experienced mountaineers. Nevertheless, the expedition ended in disaster when the party was struck by a deadly avalanche.

Eighteen-year-old Sarki Tamang was a young porter on the Kang Guru expedition. He experienced the avalanche disaster firsthand:

"The team came back down in the afternoon, and as they were tired from the climb and it was snowing, most of them were in their tents. We were preparing tea for the exhausted climbers when all of a sudden we heard a loud noise and within seconds we were blown to the side of an avalanche."

Survivors Speak

▶ Mount Kang Guru (or Kusum Kanguru) is in the Khumbu region of the Himalayas. Its name means "three snow-white gods" and refers to the mountain's triple peaks.

Mount Kang Guru

The Right Time

The Kang Guru expedition was led by French mountaineer Daniel Stolzenburg. Apart from the six other climbers, the team included 11 Nepali mountain guides and cooks. A group of 38 porters carried all their equipment. The expedition set off to Kang Guru from the nearest town in early October, in good weather conditions. The period between September and November is a good time to climb the Himalayas because by then the heavy monsoon rains have finished and the winter rains have not yet started.

Large numbers of local porters are often employed to carry heavy equipment, such as tents and supplies, on the mountain expeditions in Nepal.

The steep ridges of Kang Guru are classic avalanche terrain, with high snowfall and steep slopes.

Setting Up Base Camp

The porters set up base camp around 1.5 miles (2.5 km) below the summit, before leaving the team. This was where the team would spend time getting used to living at high altitudes. On the morning of October 20, the climbers and guides set off from base camp up the mountain but had to return by the afternoon because of unexpected heavy snow storms. While they were resting, the avalanche struck.

11

DANGER SPOT

The climbers set up base camp above a deep gorge under a rocky ridge, which they hoped would help to protect them from cold winds and snowstorms. On October 20, a snowstorm started that quickly dumped a layer of powdery snow on the slopes above the camp. The snow soon became unstable, and a sluff avalanche sped down at around 125 miles (200 km) per hour and swept the entire camp into the valley below.

The only fast way for rescue teams to reach disaster areas is by helicopter, but flights can only take place when weather conditions are safe.

The Survivors

There were just four survivors. These were cooks, who had been in a kitchen tent. As the avalanche thundered through the camp, they were blasted to the side by air and snow. All the team's equipment was carried away, including their boots. The cooks searched desperately for survivors, but realized they needed help, so they walked barefoot for 4 hours through the snow to the nearest village.

The Avalanche and the Aftermath

OCT 10, 2005
The porters and team set up base camp at 13,943 feet (4,250 m). They erect the tents and get used to the altitude in preparation for the climb to the summit of Mount Kang Guru.

OCT 18, 2005
Heavy rain falls over this part of the Himalayas. Weather stations record 8 inches (20 cm) of rain falling in 24 hours in the city of Siddharthanagar. The rain continues for the next 36 hours.

OCT 19, 2005
Fine weather prompts the team to climb higher. Snow falls.

OCT 20, 2005
The team reaches 18,700 feet (5,700 m), but heavy snow forces them back to base camp.

4:00 p.m.
An avalanche starts up in the mountain. It rips through the camp, taking everything with it.

8:30 p.m.
The four surviving porters walk barefoot to the village of Meta.

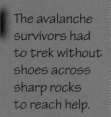
Survivors Speak

Padam Ghale was the leader of the Himalayan Rescue Association that led a rescue party to Kang Guru in 2005:

"We dug about 11.5 feet (3.5 m) at base camp, but in the gorge below, where we expected to find the remaining bodies, the snow is about 50 feet (15 m) deep."

Rescue Attempts

A search and rescue team was organized by the Himalayan Rescue Association, but bad weather stopped them from getting to the site for several days. Later, a French rescue team flew in and tried to locate any survivors, but the victims had been carried hundreds of feet by the avalanche deep into the valley below. A few bodies were found, but the rest could not be recovered until the following summer when the snows had melted.

OCT 21, 2005
A search and rescue team is put together by the Himalayan Rescue Association in Manang, the closest town to the disaster. However, bad weather prevents the team from getting close to the camp.

OCT 23, 2005
The rescue team flies to Meta. Three of the surviving porters are flown to Kathmandu for medical treatment. One remains to guide the search team.

OCT 24, 2005
The search and rescue team reaches base camp. No survivors are found.

OCT 25, 2005
One body is found; the other 17 climbers are declared dead, but still not found.

NOV 5, 2005
The search is then postponed because of bad winter weather.

JUNE 12, 2006
The remaining bodies are found after the snow melts under the hot summer sun.

WET SNOW AVALANCHES

Warm weather can increase the likelihood of avalanches happening. As the sun melts the surface snow, water trickles down through the slab. This makes the slab heavier and weakens the bonds between the layers of snow. Wet weather can have the same effect. As the rain soaks into the snow, it makes it much heavier, increasing the likelihood that it will break away from the layer of snow beneath and then slip down the mountainside as a wet snow avalanche.

Wet snow avalanches easily knock down sections of forest. The destruction an avalanche has caused is clear once the snow has melted.

Danger Signs

There are some signs that tell a skier that a wet snow avalanche might occur. The first is if the skier sinks into wet snow up to the ankles while standing on skis. If the skier squeezes a handful of snow and water drips out, this is another sign that a wet slab avalanche may take place if they ski in the area.

In 1954, an avalanche destroyed the town of Blons in the far west of Austria. Rescue workers hurried to the site to help the injured. Nine hours later, a second avalanche thundered down the mountain and hit the town, burying the rescue workers. More than 200 people died in the two disasters.

When spring sunshine melts thick snow, the snow becomes heavy with water. This can then lead to a wet snow avalanche.

Sticky Avalanche

Wet avalanches move much more slowly than dry slab avalanches. A typical speed is around 20 miles (32 km) per hour, which is around the speed of a fast sprinter. The wet snow is dense and slushy. It sticks to soil, boulders, trees, and other debris as it moves over them, and picks them up. The debris it carries along makes the wet avalanche even thicker and heavier, and slows it down even more.

CHAPTER TWO

WHAT CAUSES AVALANCHES?

Snow cover in cold, mountainous areas is made of many layers of snow, which together form the snowpack. First, one fall of snow covers the bare ground. Then, later, another snowfall covers the first layer of snow, and so on. As the layers of snow build up, the top layers press down harder on the layers underneath.

Experienced mountain walkers can learn to spot the signs that a snowpack is about to slip.

SNOW LAYERS

Snow may fall as fluffy flakes, but the flakes change shape as they are pressed down by overlying layers of snow, and by changes in temperature. In warmer weather, snowflakes can partly melt and refreeze, forming strong layers. In cold weather, the meltwater or rain can create bigger, weaker ice crystals that form weak layers in the snowpack. Most avalanches start in the weak layers that have become buried under subsequent layers of snow. When the weight above becomes too great, or if there is a slight movement, the crystals in a weak layer of snow give way and no longer attach to the overlying layer. The overlying layers then break away and form an avalanche.

WORLD'S WORST

The deadliest avalanche in Canada happened in 1910. Two trains were stranded by heavy blizzards in the Cascade Mountains. Thunderstorms made thick snow on the mountains above very wet and heavy. A giant chunk of wet snow and rock around half a mile (800 m) wide ripped off and buried the trains. This wet snow avalanche killed nearly 100 passengers.

Listening for Danger

People walking on firm snow can sometimes hear a slight hollow sound. This may mean there is empty space underneath. Sometimes it is possible to hear lower snow layers collapsing. Cracks on the surface layer can also show that lower layers are shifting and collapsing.

Snowpack layers build up over time with fresh snowfalls and changing temperatures. Together they form a record of the weather conditions in an area over days, weeks, and months.

STARTING AVALANCHES

Avalanches are triggered by a variety of things that put stress on the weak layers in the snowpack. Sometimes, just a few extra pounds of weight on top of the snowpack can make the difference between tons of snow sliding down in an avalanche or staying still. Even a wild animal padding across the snow can be all it takes to trigger an avalanche!

A snowmobile with a rider can weigh well over 650 pounds (300 kg) and travel fast enough to leave the ground and land heavily on the snowpack.

Human Triggers

In around 90 percent of avalanche incidents, the victims or someone in their party actually triggered the avalanche that affected the group. Walking, snowboarding, skiing, or snowmobiling across unstable slopes can all trigger avalanches. These activities put stress on weak layers of snow by adding weight and causing vibrations. These vibrations can be enough to topple weak layers of snow. Loud noises, such as the moving tracks of snowmobiles, also create vibrations, as do the explosions used to clear snow from areas of ski resorts.

Although snowboarders are very light, their movements can be enough to make a snowpack break away and slide down the mountainside.

Angle Matters

Whether something triggers an avalanche or not depends partly on the angle of the slope. Snow does not build up on the steepest slopes (nearest to vertical), and it does not generally slip on the shallowest slopes. Most avalanches happen on slopes with angles between 25 and 55 degrees. The snowpack tends to shift only when it gets wet and heavy at low angles.

REAL-LIFE SCIENCE
SIACHEN AVALANCHE
Kashmir, April 2012

In the spring of 2012, a Pakistan military camp in the mountains of Kashmir was suddenly engulfed in an avalanche. Although the soldiers stationed there were trained to deal with avalanches, many lost their lives.

Many more troops have been killed by avalanches during the conflict in Kashmir than by enemy fire.

Remote Region

The Siachen region is high and remote. Some parts are as high as 22,000 feet (6,700 m) above sea level. In winter, temperatures can dip to -58°F (-50°C), and the average snowfall is 35 feet (10 m). Few people would normally live and work in such extreme conditions. However, Siachen lies on the border between India and Pakistan. The two countries are in a long-running dispute over control of the region. This has led to armed conflict at times, and each country has thousands of troops patrolling this mountainous region.

Warning Signs

A Pakistani military base was established at Gayari, near the base of the Siachen glacier. The soldiers stationed there were the 6th Northern Light Infantry division. All had been trained to operate in mountains and to survive in avalanches—although it was thought the base was out of the danger zone for avalanches. However, during the especially cold and snowy winter of 2011 and 2012 in Kashmir, there were many avalanches in Siachen. Over 20 troops died in avalanches in the high mountains above the Siachen valley. Then, in the spring of 2012, the ice and snow started to thaw and rainstorms soaked into the snowpack.

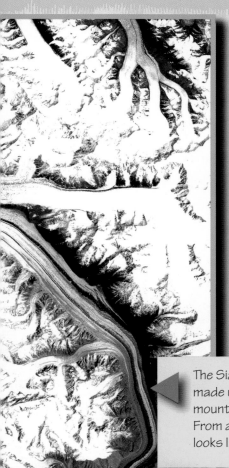

The Siachen landscape is made up of many snowy mountains and a glacier. From above, the glacier looks like a dirty river.

Shaukat Qadir is a retired Pakistani soldier who had been stationed at Siachen in the past and knew the dangers of avalanches:

"When you walk on this terrain you never know when it would come down, and certainly you cannot predict an avalanche."

Survivors Speak

Siachen is known as the world's highest battleground, where troops from India and Pakistan defend their territories.

GIANT SNOW WAVE

Around 6:00 a.m., a giant avalanche started high in the mountains above Gayari. It pushed a wave of boulders, mud, and snow in front of it. The wave completely buried the camp in a layer of snow and rubble around 70 feet (21 m) thick over an area of 0.3 square miles (1 sq km). Just as the avalanche struck, a warning message was received by the nearest large Pakistan army base, but after that, nothing more was heard from Gayari.

Rescue workers had to use snowplows and other vehicles to try to dig out survivors because the snow and ice had set so hard.

The Gayari Avalanche Rescue Operation

APRIL 7, 2012
6:00 a.m.
An ice avalanche hits Gayari, burying the camp. Some 150 soldiers and equipment are airlifted in for the search and rescue.

APRIL 8, 2012
After a night of bad weather, rescue teams resume the search.

APRIL 9, 2012
300 rescuers are now at work at the avalanche site. They manage to clear an area of around 30 x 40 feet (9 x 12 m) and 10 feet (3 m) deep. Eight US military search and rescue organizers reach Pakistan. They help the team of 300 Pakistani rescuers.

APRIL 10, 2012
There are now around 450 rescuers at work, including US and European specialist teams. They use nine heavy excavators to clear snow at five points in the area affected by the avalanche where victims are most likely to be found.

APRIL 12, 2012
Rescuers start to dig a tunnel under the snow and ice to the place where the accommodation block at the camp was sited. This is where most of the soldiers are expected to be found.

Rescue Efforts

Later that day, Pakistani military rescue teams flew to Gayari by helicopter. It was soon clear that all 124 soldiers and 11 civilians who had been at the camp were missing. The rescuers brought along rescue dogs trained to smell people buried under snow and diggers to help dig out survivors. But excavation was slow because the avalanche had set as hard as concrete when the snow and mud froze into ice. It took two days to clear a patch just the size of a small swimming pool. Rescue efforts were also slowed by bad weather that prevented further diggers and rescue teams from the United States, Germany, and Switzerland from being flown in. It was soon clear that there were no survivors, but the rescue mission continued in the hope of finding bodies.

Rescue dogs searched the snow, looking for any survivors.

APRIL 17, 2012
Rescue workers continue to dig tunnels into the snow. However, operations are slowed because poisonous gases have built up under the snow, from chemicals and waste that were buried along with the soldiers. Warmer weather increases the likelihood of further avalanches in the surrounding mountains.

APRIL 19, 2012
The Norwegian rescue team completes a survey using its specialist radar search equipment. This uses radio waves to locate buried weapons, vehicles, and other equipment under the snow that might be found near soldiers. They study the data to establish where any survivors, or bodies, might be located.

MAY 27, 2012
The first bodies are recovered from underneath the snow and rubble left by the avalanche.

THE EFFECT OF WEATHER

The speed at which the weight of snow builds up is by far the biggest factor in putting stress on weaker layers in a snowpack. Avalanches are most common during the 24 hours right after a snowstorm that has deposited 12 inches (30 cm) or more of fresh snow on a mountain's slopes.

Snow Builds Up

Rapid buildup of snow on a mountainside is the key contributor to an avalanche. If snow builds up quickly it is more likely to be unstable. A buildup of around 1 inch (2 cm) per hour is enough to produce unstable conditions. A buildup of 11 inches (30 cm) of snow in 24 hours is an extremely dangerous situation.

The snow on this huge mountain ridge has built up on the right-hand side, blown by winds as it fell. The avalanche risk for these climbers is therefore greater on the right of the ridge than on the left.

Blown by the Wind

Strong winds in mountains can cause avalanches. This is because they can quickly blow snow into heavy piles that put pressure on the snowpack. Blizzards, which are severe snowstorms with strong winds, can deposit snow on a slope 10 times faster than snow falling in low winds.

Surface Changes

Changes to the surface of the snowpack can cause avalanche problems in the future. For example, on clear, freezing nights when the air is damp, a frosting of ice crystals can appear over surfaces, including snow. These can create a slippery layer when covered by new snow.

Strong winds can blow falling snow horizontally, which makes it collect faster on slopes.

25

CHAPTER THREE
AVALANCHE IMPACTS

When an avalanche strikes, anyone caught in its path will obviously attempt to escape. In the case of a slab avalanche, they may try to get off the moving snow slab. If it is a sluff avalanche, a skier or snowboarder will probably try to outrun the avalanche. However, the snow usually moves much faster than any person can.

Avalanche survivors say the experience is what they imagine it would be like inside a huge tumble dryer full of snow and ice.

CAUGHT BY AN AVALANCHE

Avalanches often contain many tons of moving snow. When this hits someone, they are spun around in the snow, and fall over. If this happens, it is important that they try to get to the surface of the snow to avoid being buried. However, it is easy to become confused over which way is up. The air above an avalanche is often white with snowflakes blown by the moving huge mass of snow.

In the Snow

An avalanche often carries debris down the slopes, as well as snow. The debris may include boulders, trees, and soil, which

WORLD'S WORST

In 1979, a series of avalanches crashed through the Lahaul Valley in the Himalayas, killing more than 200 victims. The avalanche was triggered by blizzard conditions of wind and snow, which resulted in deep drifts of snow over the mountain foothills.

can knock into anyone caught in the avalanche's path. It may also include hazards such as broken wood and glass from buildings, and unprotected electrical wires that can cause electrical shocks or burns. It is a very dangerous place to be.

An avalanches moves
so quickly and with
such force that it is
almost impossible
for a skier to get
out of its path.

TRAPPED

Anyone who gets caught by an avalanche often ends up being buried under snow. Snow can be so heavy that it can crush a person. It can also make someone so cold that they suffer from hypothermia. This is a condition in which a person's body temperature drops dangerously low. However, around two-thirds of avalanche victims die from suffocation because they do not have enough oxygen to breathe under the snow.

Rescuers carefully press a long pole into the snow to try to find any survivors buried beneath it.

Air Supply

How well avalanche victims can breathe depends partly on the type of snow in the avalanche. People buried under light, fluffy snow may be able to breathe oxygen from air trapped around the snowflakes. Victims that get caught up in avalanches of wet, heavy snow have less chance of being able to breathe because the snow contains less air. It is also heavier, making any attempt to move much harder.

WORLD'S WORST

On September 20, 2002, the Russian actor Sergei Bodrov Jr. was shooting a film in the mountains of the northern Caucasus, Russia, when a 20-million-ton (18 million tonne) avalanche fell from the northern slope of the Kazbekmassif. Known as the Kolka-Karmadon rock-ice slide, it killed Bodrov, the 27 members of the movie crew, and 98 other people.

Breathing Time

Studies of avalanche survival show that the quicker a person is rescued, the more likely they are to survive. Over 90 percent of avalanche victims survive if they are dug out within 15 minutes. After 45 minutes, only 30 percent of victims survive. The longer a person is buried, the more oxygen they use up from gaps in the snow around their face. They also breathe out more and more carbon dioxide, which is poisonous in large amounts. Avalanche experts tell people to make an air pocket in front of their mouth within seconds of being trapped to increase their chance of survival.

Rescuers search for any sign of avalanche victims. These include belongings such as clothing which may have been ripped off as the victim was caught up in the snow.

REAL-LIFE SCIENCE
STEVENS PASS, WASHINGTON STATE, 2012

Stevens Pass, near Seattle, is one of the most popular outdoor recreation areas in Washington State, in the far northwest of the United States. Many skiers come here to enjoy backcountry skiing in the beautiful landscape filled with snowy mountains and deep forests. However, in February 2012, it was the scene of a fatal avalanche that resulted in the deaths of three skiers.

Backcountry skiers are often in remote places when an avalanche strikes, making rescue even more difficult.

Stevens Pass

Stevens Pass is in the Cascade Mountains, which run north to south through Washington State, in the far northwest of the United States.

In the Morning

The morning of Sunday, February 20, 2012, was bright and warm, and ideal skiing weather. Around 2 feet (60 cm) of fresh, powdery snow lay on the ground, and large numbers of visitors were expected at the Stevens Pass resort. A group of 12 skiers set off into a backcountry area named Tunnel Creek, up above Stevens Pass, to get away from the crowds. They knew that the Northwest Weather and Avalanche Center had issued a warning for high avalanche danger for areas such as Tunnel Creek that were above 5,000 feet (1,700 m).

The Avalanche Hits

The party split into three groups of four. In one group, the skiers were taking turns skiing down a section of mountain. That way, if an avalanche started, only one person in the group might be affected. Three of the group waited downhill among the trees. In the event of an avalanche, this is a safer place than on an open slope because people can hold on to trees to stop themselves from being swept away. The fourth skier triggered a slab avalanche around 30 feet (10 m) wide. It carried him down the slope, but also pulled the other three away from the trees.

Elyse Saugstad is a professional skier from Alaska who got caught in the Stevens Pass avalanche:

"There wasn't much sound. I was just trying to figure out within seconds what exactly was happening and how I was going to deal with this. It was a very long ride and there was a lot of time to think."

The views at Stevens Pass are breathtaking. However, the terrain can be treacherous.

SWEPT AWAY

The avalanche carried all four skiers around 3,000 feet (1,000 m) down the slope and into a gorge. Professional skier Elyse Saugstad was among the four skiers swept away. She was wearing a backpack containing an avalanche airbag. The avalanche moved so fast that she had very little time to react, but her first thought was to activate the device.

Many backcountry skiers wear an avalanche airbag to protect them in the event of an avalanche.

Saved by an Airbag

Although Elyse was buried in the snow during the long slide down the mountainside, the airbag brought her to the surface. This meant that she was able to keep her head and hands free of snow, and thus survive the avalanche. Of all the four skiers caught up in the avalanche, only Elyse had an avalanche airbag.

The Stevens Pass Avalanche as It Happened

FEBRUARY 17, 2012
A powerful winter storm hits Stevens Pass ski resort in Washington State. The resort reports 26 inches (66 cm) of fresh snow falling over the next 48 hours, over half of it falling on the night of February 18.

FEB 19, 2012 9:00 a.m.
Team members arrive and ski in the fenced area at Stevens Pass. The Northwest Weather and Avalanche Center issues a high avalanche danger warning.

11:00 a.m.
A team of 12 skiers decide to head into the dangerous area to ski. They split into several small groups and make sure that they only ski across possible avalanche slopes singly. Other members of the group wait among trees,

knowing the trees could offer some protection from the moving snow if an avalanche were to strike in the area.
.
11:50 a.m.
An avalanche strikes near the seventh skier crossing a slope. It is approximately 2,650 feet (900 m) long, 200 feet (65 m) wide,

A Tragedy Unfolds

The remaining members of the group skied down the slope after the avalanche. They all turned on their transceivers, which are special radio receivers that can be used to locate other beacons nearby, including those carried by missing people. Elyse was fine and at the surface, but the other three skiers were buried. The group used their portable shovels to dig down and find their missing friends. Sadly, they were not breathing, and attempts to revive them failed. The victims had died from a lack of air under the snow.

Airbag systems have a handle on one of the straps. Pulling the handle releases gas from a canister that fills the bag in seconds.

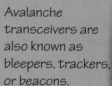

Avalanche transceivers are also known as bleepers, trackers, or beacons.

and 32 inches (1 m) deep. The avalanche sweeps three other skiers, including Elyse Saugstad, from among trees and down the slope.

11:51 a.m.
The avalanche comes to a standstill. Elyse and others caught in the avalanche have been swept hundreds of feet downslope. Other members of the team turn on their transceivers in the hope of locating the missing skiers. They then start skiing down the slope.

12:01 p.m.
Other team members locate and start to excavate Elyse, who is visible above the snow, having been lifted above the snow by her avalanche airbag.

12:02 p.m.
The Stevens Pass emergency team is alerted and sent for. By the time they arrive the skiers have found the three avalanche victims. One is buried a few feet from Elyse and the others 50 feet (16 m) and around 300 feet (100 m) away. None of the victims had been wearing an airbag.

RESCUE TEAMS

Avalanche survivors or witnesses often call out specialist rescue teams. These teams usually know where avalanches might happen in the local mountains, and they are specially trained to find and assist buried people. They try to get to the avalanche site as quickly as possible, often by helicopter, because the longer victims are buried, the less likely they are to survive.

Rescue teams are trained to quickly check the disater area with poles and devices that can detect survivors.

Searching for Victims

Rescuers use various methods to find people buried in the snow. The victims are then dug out with shovels or sometimes mechanical diggers:

- The rescuers look for clues about where people might be buried, such as piles of snow with debris mixed in.
- They walk together slowly, spread out in a line, and press long poles into the snow every 20 inches (50 cm) to feel if there is anything solid underneath.
- They use avalanche transceivers or beacons to detect signals from other buried transceivers.
- They use devices that can detect body heat underground.
- They listen for muffled sounds or even calls for help from beneath the snow.

WORLD'S WORST

Snowboarders are often the victims of avalanches. The vibrations caused by the boarders can trigger an avalanche. In 2009, three-quarters of the people killed by avalanches in western Canada were snowboarders.

One avalanche rescue dog can search an area for buried survivors 8 times faster than a line of 20 people probing poles into the snow.

Rescue Dogs

Search and rescue teams use trained dogs, such as German Shepherds, to find people buried under snow. People always produce a slight smell because of the bacteria that grows on their skin, and dogs can smell this far better than people can. A rescue dog can usually smell a person buried 12 feet (4 m) under snow, but sometimes the dog can locate people buried twice this deep.

Dogs have 40 times more smell receptors in their nose than people, making their sense of smell far more powerful.

CHAPTER FOUR
CONTROLLING AVALANCHES

There are a number of ways that people can prepare for avalanches. Scientists at avalanche institutes work to predict when they are likely to happen. One way is to examine photographs of clouds taken by satellites in space to spot wet weather that may lead to snowfall. Scientists combine this data with records of past snowfall, current wind direction, and air temperature to predict when snow might build up fast enough to become unstable and create avalanches.

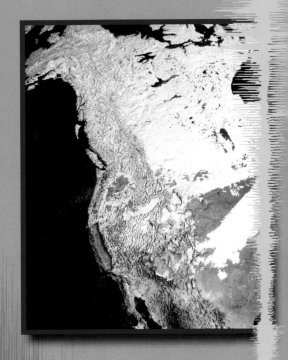

Satellite images are a vital piece of information in forecasting weather and avalanche risk.

PREDICTING AVALANCHES

Scientists visit areas of deep snow to check the stability of the snowpack. They carefully dig holes, called "snowpits," and measure the depths of the different layers of snow. They also examine the type of snow in each layer using electronic probes that measure water content and strength. Using a snow saw, they cut vertical blocks out of the snowpack at the edges of the snowpit. Then they tap and pull on the blocks to see how easily they collapse or come away from the underlying snow. This gives them an idea of how likely it is that an avalanche will happen in that area.

WORLD'S WORST

In 1972, a climbing team from South Korea attempted to climb Mount Manaslu in Nepal. The climbing expedition ended in disaster when an avalanche buried the climbers' camp. It killed 15 climbers, including 10 porters.

Scientists use weather stations, such as this one near the Haystack Creek avalanche path in Montana, to help them predict avalanches.

AVALANCHES AND FORESTS

Trees on mountains help to prevent avalanches. Their strong roots hold the soil and snow together, making them less likely to slide when wet. Woods or forests also form a natural barrier that can stop, or at least slow down, some avalanches. They can even change the direction of an avalanche, diverting it away from a village. Trees are individually very strong and flexible and can withstand the impact of strong winds. However, even the largest trees cannot withstand a big, fast avalanche as it crashes down a mountainside carrying with it hundreds of tons of snow and ice.

Planting trees on slopes is one way to help prevent avalanches. Trees catch a lot of avalanche snow and so help reduce the destruction it causes.

Tree Laws

In mountain areas in some countries, there are laws preventing people from clearing forests on slopes due to their importance in preventing avalanches. In fourteenth-century Switzerland, people faced a death sentence for clearing forests without permission.

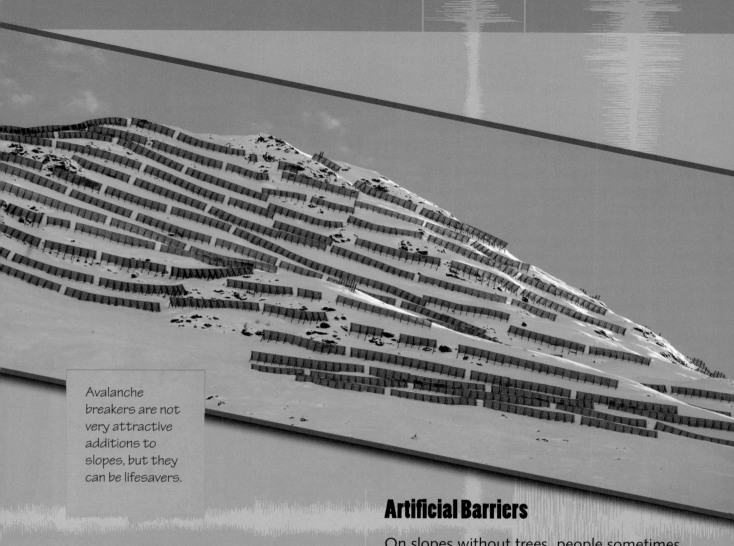

Avalanche breakers are not very attractive additions to slopes, but they can be lifesavers.

WORLD'S WORST

On Thursday, July 12, 2012, nine of a party of 28 mountain climbers were killed in France when an avalanche hit them. The climbers were making an ascent of Mount Maudit in the French Alps when a huge wall of ice and snow hit them and swept them off the mountainside.

Artificial Barriers

On slopes without trees, people sometimes put up barriers called avalanche breakers. These strong metal or concrete fences are bolted firmly into the rock. They are designed to trap snow, which prevents it from slipping down a mountainside.

It is not possible, however, to install barriers on every bare slope, especially in remote regions, because it is so expensive. Instead, scientists create maps that mark the places where avalanches are most likely to happen. Engineers then decide where to install the avalanche breakers to provide protection.

DANGEROUS WORK

Snow becomes a hazard once it has built up into unstable, thick snowpacks. Ski rangers regularly walk or ski across snow ridges in mountainous areas. As they travel, they check the strength of snow by zigzagging across it on skis or jumping on the snow. They also look out for rocky ridges where thick snow is overhanging the slope below.

Even looking for signs of potential avalanches is highly dangerous. Rangers are trained to do their job as safely as possible.

Working Safely

Ski rangers work in pairs—one tests the snow while the other watches from a safe spot. Both rangers carry electronic transceivers. They also anchor themselves to a tree or boulder before testing dangerous areas. Sometimes ski rangers purposely cause avalanches, or "break" the snow, to make areas safer.

WORLD'S WORST

Thousands of soldiers lost their lives to avalanches while fighting in the Italian Alps during World War I. Some people think the number killed may be as many as 80,000. Some of the avalanches were caused accidentally when shells fired at the enemy hit snow-covered slopes.

Using Explosives

One way to break snow is to blow it up. Ski rangers plant explosives in the snow and then detonate them from a safe distance. They may also fire explosive shells at slopes using special guns called avalaunchers. By breaking the snow, they can prevent it building up into a potential avalanche.

Explosions by Helicopter

Rangers sometimes use a helicopter to break snow. The helicopter flies over the exact spot where the avalanche needs to be started. Then it lowers a large metal cone, called a daisy bell, down onto the snow. Inside the bell, gases are set alight to cause an explosion. This creates a shock wave that vibrates in the snow for a distance of around 45 feet (15 m).

These ski rangers are practicing with explosives. In a real situation, they would stand farther away to make sure they were not caught by the moving snow of a slab avalanche.

41

LIVING IN AVALANCHE AREAS

People who live in snowy mountain areas expect avalanches and prepare for the worst in different ways. Highways and railroad tracks under exposed slopes are often covered by galleries. These are tunnels that stop the vehicles and people inside them from being covered with snow, ice, and other debris if an avalanche strikes.

Carrying a backpack with emergency equipment, such as an airbag or a transceiver, could make the difference between life and death in an avalanche.

WORLD'S WORST

In 1991, an avalanche descended on several towns in Bingol, Turkey. An enormous wave of snow and debris swept down a local mountainside and piled into the towns below. The snow flattened buildings, killing a total of 225 people.

Survival Preparation

People in avalanche-prone areas learn key avalanche survival techniques:

- Call once: This is to alert anyone nearby. The person should then close the mouth to avoid breathing in too much snow.
- Drop equipment: The weight and size of ski or board equipment and snowmobiles can drag a person down a mountain slope and also cause injuries.

Buildings in avalanche areas have long, sloping roofs. If an avalanche strikes, it is more likely to pass over the house rather than knock it down.

- Swim and grab: The person should move their arms and legs as if swimming, to try to stay near the surface of the avalanche snow. They should try to grab any nearby trees to escape the avalanche.
- Make space: Snow will build up tightly around a person if they stop moving, so they must cup a hand or arm over their mouth to make an air pocket.
- Be seen: The person should try to thrust an arm or leg up through the snow so rescuers can see them.
- Stay calm: This is very difficult, but essential, because people breathe air more slowly when they are calm.

AVOIDING DANGER

The best way to avoid an avalanche is to stay away from places where they might strike. It is safer to travel above an avalanche area than through it. It is also important to avoid avalanche paths. These are land shapes, such as gullies, bowls, and open slopes, on or in which sliding snow can travel fast or funnel downward.

Parts of a mountain that have large hollows, such as this one, are more likely to be avalanche sites.

Avalanche Forecasts

People visiting snowy areas should listen out for avalanche forecasts. Most countries use computerized warning systems that are constantly updated with new weather data and are used to warn people of avalanche risks. Forecasts use the experience of ski rangers and mountain experts who know the area and how the snow has been building up. Many mountain parks and ski resorts now have hotlines and web pages with the very latest avalanche forecasts.

Future Avalanches

Avalanche risk or frequency in a place varies from year to year, depending on the weather. Global weather patterns are changing as a result of global warming. Temperature changes will probably affect snowfall, rainfall, and the stability of snowpacks in mountainous areas. This could create more avalanches in the future.

WORLD'S WORST

In 1965, a huge ice chunk broke off from a glacier in Switzerland and buried the construction site of the Mattmark Dam. The avalanche killed 88 construction workers.

Signs are there for a reason. Watch out for avalanche warnings!

DANGER OF AVALANCHE
STOP
DANGER OF AVALANCHE

GLOSSARY

air pocket: a space around a person when they get buried that contains air they can breathe to keep them alive

avalanche airbag: an inflatable balloon in a backpack. It carries someone caught in an avalanche to the surface

avalanche institute: a place where scientists study what makes avalanches happen and learn how to predict and prevent avalanches

backcountry: remote, isolated, and unpopulated area of wild countryside

bacteria: tiny living things that live in soil, water, and air, and on or in the tissues of plants, people, and animals

debris: in avalanches, pieces of material, such as trees, rocks, and fences, that get mixed in with the snow

detonate: to set off explosives

earthquake: a huge release of energy that happens when parts of the rock layer beneath Earth's surface suddenly slip against each other

forecast: to predict what might happen in the future, such as weather changes

glacier: a slowly moving river of ice more than 150 feet (50 m) thick. Most glaciers grow faster than they melt.

gorge: a deep valley between cliffs made by a river wearing away the rocks

hypothermia: when a person's body temperature drops too low for normal body functions to continue

meltwater: water formed when ice melts. This often happens in the spring.

satellite: object in orbit around Earth that collects and sends information, such as images, or is used for communication

slab avalanche: when a thick layer of snow breaks off and slides downhill

sluff avalanche: when a mass of loose snow moves rapidly downhill

snowpack: layers of snow that fell at different times over an area of ground

snowpit: a hole dug in the snowpack so that scientists can examine its layers

summit: the peak or top of a mountain

transceiver: a type of radio that can send out and receive signals. One transceiver can locate a second using the strength of signal it receives.

trigger: to start something off, such as an avalanche. Avalanches may be triggered by extra weight, movements, such as vibrations, and sounds.

vibrations: rapid movements to and fro

wet avalanche: when heavy, wet snow slides down a mountain slope

FOR MORE INFORMATION

Books

Green, Jen. *Stories About Surviving Natural Disasters*. London, UK: Franklin Watts, 2010.

Oxlade, Chris. *Mountain Rescue*. Chicago, IL: Raintree, 2012.

Shone, Rob. *Avalanches and Landslides*. New York, NY: Rosen Publishing Group, 2007.

Vogler, Sara and Jan Burchett. *Avalanche Alert*. North Mankato, MN: Stone Arch Books, 2012.

Websites

Learn lots of information about recent US avalanches, including data on survival, and use an online tutorial that shows you what different avalanche warnings mean.
www.avalanche.org

The website of the US Search and Rescue Taskforce outlines the causes and signs of avalanches and how to be prepared in avalanche areas.
www.ussartf.org/avalanches.htm

Learn how you can create different types of avalanche by changing precipitation, temperature, and wind.
environment.nationalgeographic.com/environment/natural-disasters/avalanche-interactive/

INDEX